MW00947164

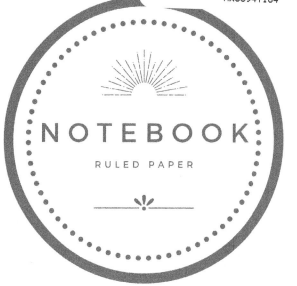

NOTEBOOK

RULED PAPER

THIS BOOK BELONGS TO:

Copyright © 2020 All rights reserved.
authored by: Marcel Doll, Hammerschbüchel 10, 53797 Lohmar, Germany

Made in the USA
Las Vegas, NV
10 January 2022

41032848R10069